rockschool®

Piano Grade 3

Performance pieces, technical exercises, supporting tests and in-depth guidance for Rockschool examinations

For more information, turn to page 5

www.rslawards.com

Acknowledgements

Published by Rockschool Ltd. © 2015
Catalogue Number RSK200004
ISBN: 978-1-908920-83-6
27 June 2016 | Errata details can be found at *www.rslawards.com*

SYLLABUS
Syllabus written and devised by Nik Preston
Syllabus consultants: Hannah Vasanth, Julia Martin, Stuart Slater, Jono Harrison, Simon Troup and Jennie Troup
Hit tune arrangements by Jono Harrison and Nik Preston
Supporting tests written by Jono Harrison, Nik Preston, Ash Preston and Hannah Vasanth
Piano arrangements of Rockschool compositions by Brian Henry
Syllabus advisors: Mary Keene, Patrick Healy, Emily Nash, Dan Phelps and Mike Stylianou

PUBLISHING
Fact Files written by Julia Martin, Joe Bennett, Charlie Griffiths, Stephen Lawson, Simon Pitt, Stuart Ryan and James Uings
Music engraving and book layout by Simon Troup and Jennie Troup of Digital Music Art
Proof reading and copy editing by Simon Troup, Jennie Troup, Jonathan Preiss, Mary Keene, Stuart Slater and Nik Preston
Cover design by Philip Millard
Cover photograph © Jason Kempin/Getty Images

AUDIO
Produced by Ash Preston, Jono Harrison, Brian Henry and Music Sales
Engineered by Ash Preston, Jono Harrison, Brian Henry and Music Sales
Mixed and mastered by Ash Preston
Edited by Ash Preston
Supporting Tests recorded by Ash Preston, Jono Harrison and Hannah Vasanth
Mastered by Ash Preston
Executive producers: John Simpson and Norton York

MUSICIANS
Jono Harrison, Hannah Vasanth, Brian Henry, Nik Preston, James Arben, Jason Bowld, Stuart Clayton, Andy Crompton, Neel Dhorajiwala, Fergus Gerrand, Felipe Karam, Kishon Khan, Noam Lederman, DJ Harry Love, Dave Marks, Jon Musgrave, Jake Painter, Richard Pardy, Ross Stanley, Carl Sterling, Henry Thomas, Camilo Tirado, Steve Walker, Chris Webster, Norton York, Nir Z

DISTRIBUTION
Exclusive Distributors: Music Sales Ltd

CONTACTING ROCKSCHOOL
www.rslawards.com
Telephone: +44 (0)845 460 4747
Email: *info@rslawards.com*

Table of Contents

Introductions & Information

Rockschool Grade Pieces

Technical Exercises

Supporting Tests

Additional Information

Welcome to Rockschool Piano Grade 3

Welcome to **Rockschool's 2015 Piano syllabus**. This syllabus has been designed to equip all aspiring pianists with both a diverse range of stylistically appropriate, industry relevant skills and a thoroughly engaging learning experience.

Utilising an array of well known repertoire, Rockschool's own compositions and a truly innovative range of supporting tests, the continued progression of any candidate is assured from Debut through to Grade 8. Additionally, the Rockschool compositions, which are the 4th, 5th and 6th pieces featured in each book, have been arranged for Bass, Drums, Piano and Guitar at Grades 3, 5 and 8, in order to help pianists perform repertoire in an ensemble environment where available.

The syllabus has been authored to ensure that pianists can develop as accompanists, soloists, sight readers and improvisers whilst enabling both teacher and candidate to choose the areas that they wish to specialise in.

Rockschool's long standing commitment to raising academic standards, assessing industry-relevant skills and ensuring student engagement is world renowned. The 2015 Piano syllabus has been conceived in order to build upon this success and continue the evolution of the contemporary music world's first awarding body.

When combined with **Rockschool's Popular Music Theory syllabus**, the 2015 syllabus is guaranteed to furnish every candidate with both the practical skills and theoretical understanding necessary to perform at the highest level, across a whole range of contemporary music.

Nik Preston – Head of Product Development and Publishing

Piano Exams

At each grade you have the option of taking one of two different types of examination:

- **Grade Exam**

  A Grade Exam is a mixture of music performances, technical work and tests. You are required to prepare three pieces (two of which may be Free Choice Pieces) and the contents of the Technical Exercise section. This accounts for 75% of the exam marks. The other 25% consists of: either a Sight Reading or an Improvisation & Interpretation test (10%), two Ear Tests (10%), and finally you will be asked five General Musicianship Questions (5%). The pass mark is 60%.

- **Performance Certificate**

  A Performance Certificate is equivalent to a Grade Exam, but in a Performance Certificate you are required to perform five pieces. A maximum of three of these can be Free Choice Pieces. Each song is marked out of 20 and the pass mark is 60%.

Book Contents

The book is divided into a number of sections:

- **Exam Pieces**

  In this book you will find six pieces of Grade 3 standard. Each song is preceded by a Fact File detailing information about the original recording, the composer and the artist/s who performed it. Every exam piece is notated for piano, but a selection also have the vocal melody notated. This is included as reference material and is not intended to be performed in the exam itself. In your exam you must perform to the backing tracks provided.

- **Technical Exercises**

  There are either three or four types of technical exercise, depending on the grade:
  Group A – scales
  Group B – arpeggios/broken chords
  Group C – chord voicings
  Group D – a choice of stylistic studies. Please note, Group D only exists at Grades 6–8.

- **Supporting Tests**

   You are required to undertake three kinds of unprepared, supporting test:

   1. Sight Reading or an Improvisation & Interpretation test at Debut to Grade 5.
            Please note, these are replaced by mandatory Quick Study Pieces (QSPs) at Grades 6–8.
   2. Ear Tests: Debut to Grade 3 feature Melodic Recall and Chord Recognition.
            Grades 4–8 feature Melodic Recall and Harmonic Recall.
   3. General Musicianship Questions (GMQs), which you will be asked by the examiner at the end of each exam.

   Each book features *examples* of the types of unprepared tests likely to appear in the exam.
   The examiner will give you a different version in the exam.

- **General Information**

   You will find information on exam procedures, including online examination entry, marking schemes, information on Free Choice Pieces and improvisation requirements for each grade.

Audio

In addition to the Grade book, we have also provided audio in the form of backing tracks (minus piano) and examples (including piano) for both the pieces and the supporting tests where applicable. This can be downloaded from RSL directly at *www.rslawards.com/downloads*

You will need to input this code when prompted: **X85MF8XRRH**

The audio files are supplied in MP3 format. Once downloaded you will be able to play them on any compatible device.

You can find further details about Rockschool's Piano syllabus by downloading the syllabus guide from our website: *www.rslawards.com*

All candidates should download and read the accompanying syllabus guide when using this grade book.

Piano Notation Explained

THE MUSICAL STAVE shows pitches and rhythms and is divided by lines into bars. Pitches are named after the first seven letters of the alphabet.

Grace Note: Play the grace note on or before the beat depending on the style of music, then move quickly to the note it leads onto.

Spread Chord: Play the chord from the bottom note up (top down only if there is a downward arrow head). The final note should sound by the appropriate notated bar position.

Tremolando: Oscillate at speed between marked notes.

Pedal Marking: Depress and then release the sustain pedal. Multiple pedal operations in a short space of time may be simplified as shown in the last two beats of the bar below.

Glissando: Play the notes between the notated pitches by sliding over the keyboard with the fingers or fingernails.

Finger Markings: These numbers represent your fingers. 1 is the thumb, 2 the index finger and so on.

 (accent) • Accentuate note (play it louder).

 (accent) • Accentuate note with great intensity.

 (staccato) • Shorten time value of note.

 (accent) • Accentuate note with more arm weight.

D.%. al Coda

• Go back to the sign (%), then play until the bar marked ***To Coda*** ⊕ then skip to the section marked ⊕ ***Coda***.

D.C. al Fine

• Go back to the beginning of the song and play until the bar marked ***Fine*** (end).

Una Corda

• Use soft pedal

• Repeat the bars between the repeat signs.

• When a repeated section has different endings, play the first ending only the first time and the second ending only the second time.

SONG TITLE: UNFAITHFUL

ALBUM: A GIRL LIKE ME

RELEASED: 2006

LABEL: DEF JAM, SRP

GENRE: POP/R&B

VOCALS: RIHANNA

PIANO: CARL STURKEN

STRING ARRANGEMENT: ROBERT MOUNCEY

PERCUSSION: TED HEMBERGER

WRITTEN BY: SHAFFER SMITH, MIKKEL S. ERIKSEN, TOR ERIK HERMANSEN

PRODUCED BY: STARGATE, MAKEBA RIDDICK

UK CHART PEAK: 2

This was the second single from Rihanna's second album, *A Girl Like Me*. Songwriter Shaffer Smith is better known as Ne-Yo, who has also had a string of hits both as songwriter and artist.

The track encountered some controversy because of the lyrics, although they are supposed to express regret. In an interview, Rihanna stated that "finally someone put it in perspective: girls cheat too". In response, a critic stated they were concerned that the lyrics could be interpreted as "devoid of remorse". The singer said of the song that she wanted to speak about personal experiences: "what it's like to be a girl like me".

The song is a Pop/R&B ballad. The writers created the song around the piano part as they worked. Rihanna said that singing a ballad was "new ground" for her but this turned out to be one of her favourite songs from the album.

Rihanna is originally from Bridgetown, Barbados. Producer Evan Rogers noticed her and helped her put together a demo that gained the attention of Def Jam records. The president at the time, Jay-Z signed her immediately on the night she auditioned.

Rihanna is currently one of the biggest selling artists of all time, with sales of over 41 million albums and 150 million songs worldwide. During her career she has won two BRIT awards and eight Grammys. After the success of 'Better Have My Money' in July 2015, the Recording Industry Association of America (RIAA) announced that Rihanna had become the first artist to surpass more than 100 million digital singles.

Unfaithful

Rihanna

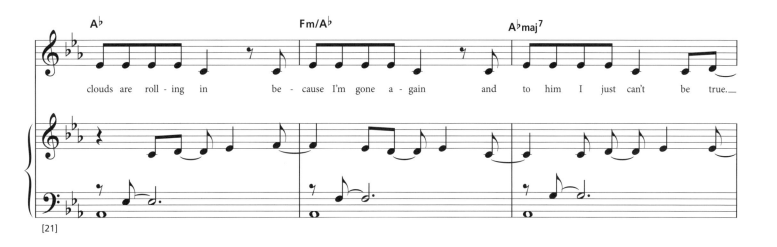

kills him___ in - side to know that I am hap - py___ with

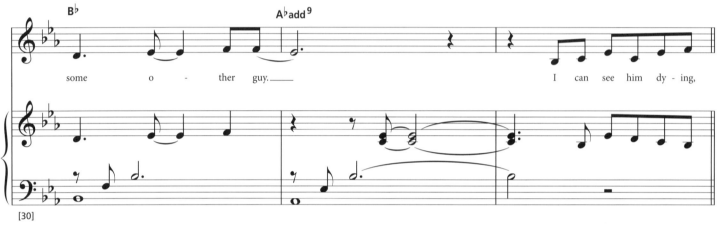

some o - ther guy.___ I can see him dy - ing,

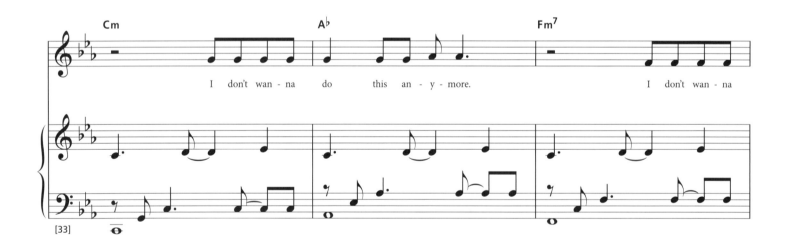

I don't wan - na do this an - y - more. I don't wan - na

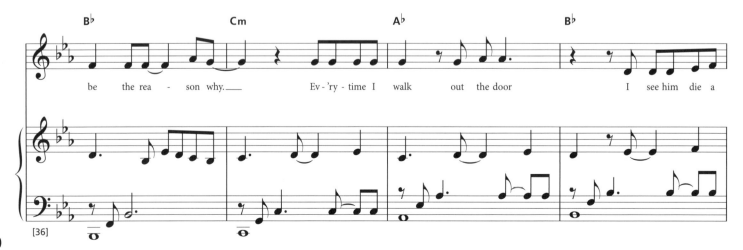

be the rea - son why.___ Ev -'ry - time I walk out the door I see him die a

SONG TITLE: SKYFALL

RELEASED: 2012

LABEL: XL, COLUMBIA

GENRE: ORCHESTRAL POP

VOCALS: ADELE

PIANO: NIKOLAJ TORP LARSEN

GUITAR: JAMES REID

DRUMS: LEO TAYLOR

BASS: TOM HERBERT

CHOIR: METRO VOICES

PERCUSSION: PAUL EPWORTH

ORCHESTRA LEADER: THOMAS BOWES

WRITTEN BY: ADELE ADKINS,

PAUL EPWORTH

PRODUCED BY: PAUL EPWORTH

UK CHART PEAK: 2

The song was written as the theme tune for the 2012 James Bond film, *Skyfall* – the 23rd film in the franchise. Adele was approached by the film's producers to write the tune and after reading the script, she accepted. The producers allegedly asked her as they felt it might bring back the "classic Shirley Bassey feel" that was associated with iconic bond themes. Adele and co-writer Paul Epworth wanted to create a song that was true to the narrative, rather than the Romanticism of the film, but were originally concerned that it might be 'too dark'.

Co-writer, Paul Epworth has worked with Adele previously (on single 'Rolling in the Deep') and written with other artists such as: Florence and the Machine, Plan B and Lana Del Rey.

'Skyfall' was recorded in two sessions at the legendary Abbey Road Studios with a 77-piece orchestra, conducted by J.A.C. Redford. It received its first play on Adele's website at 0:07 GMT on the 5th October 2012; dubbed 'James Bond Day' as it marked the 50th anniversary of the release of the first ever James Bond film, *Dr. No*.

Both Epworth and Adele mention that they worked hard to incorporate elements of previous Bond themes and motifs into the composition. Producer and co-writer Epworth decided to watch all of the first thirteen Bond films to understand what he called the "musical code" of the music. He says he was looking for a way to give the song what he called the "60s jazzy quality" that typifies Bond themes.

The film won Best Single at the 2013 Brit Awards and was the first ever Bond theme to win an Oscar.

Skyfall

Adele

Words & Music by Paul Epworth & Adele Adkins
© Copyright 2012 Melted Stone Publishing Ltd.
Universal Music Publishing Limited/EMI Music Publishing Limited.

Otis Redding | The Dock Of The Bay

SONG TITLE: (SITTIN' ON) THE DOCK
OF THE BAY

ALBUM: THE DOCK OF THE BAY

RELEASED: 1968

LABEL: VOLT/ATCO

GENRE: RHYTHM & BLUES/SOUL

VOCALS: OTIS REDDING

BAND: BOOKER T AND THE MGS

GUITAR: STEVE CROPPER

BASS: DONALD "DUCK" DUNN

DRUMS: AL JACKSON JR.

KEYBOARDS: BOOKER T. JONES

WRITTEN BY: STEVE CROPPER, OTIS
REDDING

PRODUCED BY: STEVE CROPPER

UK CHART PEAK: 3

Sitt-in' in the morn - ing sun,——
Sitt-in' here rest-in' my bones,——

Redding wrote this song whilst staying on a houseboat in San Fransisco. He started the lyrics, but his writing partner and producer Steve Cropper took them and finished them stating: "Otis didn't really write about himself, but I did… Dock of the Bay was about him leaving Georgia to go out to San Fransisco to perform". The style of the song is different to his earlier work and he had been discussing a change to his songwriting style with his wife.

The band used were the 'house band' of the label Stax Records named Booker T and the MGs. They recorded for a host of artists on the label including: Bill Withers, Wilson Pickett, and Sam & Dave.

Unfortunately, Redding died in a plane crash only three days after recording this single and six weeks before its release in 1968; he was only 26 years old. It was his only number one single and also the first-ever posthumous number one single in the US, which went on to win two Grammy awards.

The inclusion of the whistling on the original track has several stories attached to it. Some have said it is because Redding didn't have a final verse written and so whistled instead. Cropper says it is because

Redding forgot the ad-lib he had planned to do at the end of the song. The beach sound effects (seagulls and waves crashing) were dubbed in after recording as Cropper remembered that Redding wanted to recreate the sounds he had heard on his houseboat.

Redding is credited with being heavily influential to Soul as a genre. It combines elements of R&B with Gospel music.

(Sittin' On) The Dock Of The Bay

Otis Redding

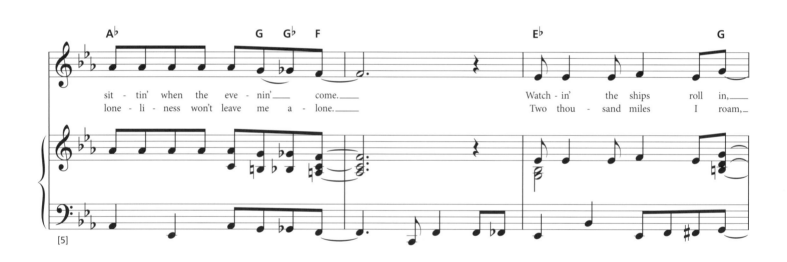

SONG TITLE: OVERRATED

GENRE: ALTERNATIVE ROCK

TEMPO: 125 BPM

KEY: E

COMPOSERS: BOB GRACEFUL

& KUNG FU DRUMMER

PERSONNEL: STUART RYAN (GTR)

HENRY THOMAS (BASS)

NOAM LEDERMAN (DRUMS)

OVERVIEW

'Overrated' is an Alt Rock track in the style of bands like Foo Fighters, Biffy Clyro and Twin Atlantic.

THE BIGGER PICTURE

Ex-Nirvana drummer and Foo Fighters frontman Dave Grohl has been central to the development of this branch of Alt Rock. While playing drums with Nirvana, Grohl began working on demo tapes that formed the basis of the Foo Fighters' first album. Their early records retained the quiet-loud dynamic of Nirvana's music while revealing Grohl's melodic songwriting.

The influence of Foo Fighters is most obvious in two contemporary alt rock groups, both of whom happen to come from the West of Scotland: Biffy Clyro and Twin Atlantic. Like the Foo Fighters, both bands have their moments of heaviness tempered by bursts of melody and chord suspension.

RECOMMENDED LISTENING

Foo Fighters have amassed dozens of songs since 1995, the best of which can be found on their *Greatest Hits* (2009). Biffy Clyro's last album *Only Revolutions* (2009) was their commercial breakthrough, but their previous record *Puzzle* (2007) bears a more obvious Foos influence. The latest album by Twin Atlantic *Free* (2011) was the subject of much critical acclaim and is a testament to Grohl and co.'s enduring legacy.

Overrated

Bob Graceful & Kung Fu Drummer

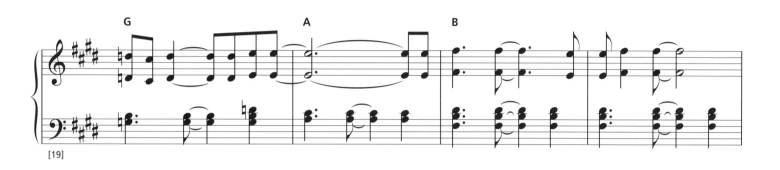

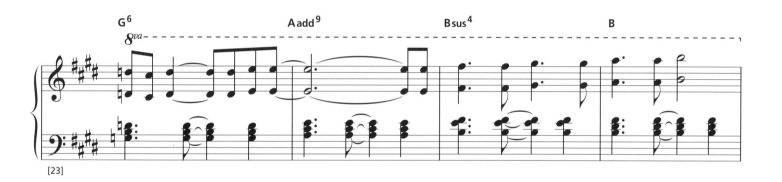

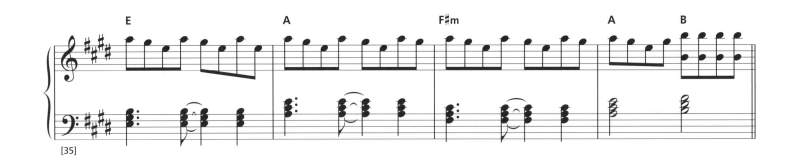

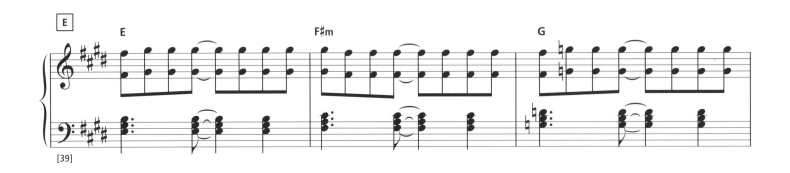

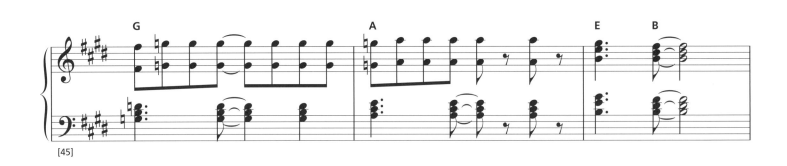

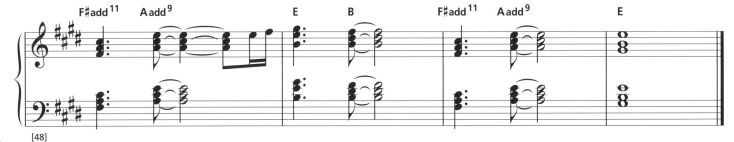

Rockschool | Rasta Monkey

SONG TITLE: RASTA MONKEY

GENRE: REGGAE

TEMPO: 156 BPM

KEY: G

COMPOSER: NOAM LEDERMAN

PERSONNEL: STUART RYAN (GTR)

HENRY THOMAS (BASS)

NOAM LEDERMAN (DRUMS)

ROSS STANLEY (KEYS)

FERGUS GERRAND (PERC)

[9]

OVERVIEW

'Rasta Monkey' is a track that brings to mind Reggae stars such as Bob Marley, Jimmy Cliff and Toots And The Maytals.

THE BIGGER PICTURE

Reggae is the music of Jamaica, and gained worldwide success and appeal through the hits of Bob Marley, who remains Reggae's undisputed superstar. The genre developed in Jamaica in the late 1960s, as a progression of its more uptempo predecessors Ska and Rocksteady. The key feature of the style is its accent on the offbeat, known as the 'skank'.

Marley and his band The Wailers are the best known exponents of the style; other pioneers include Jimmy Cliff and Toots And The Maytals. To some extent, the UK and American public weren't drawn to the genre until Eric Clapton had a top 10 hit with his cover of Marley's 'I Shot The Sheriff' in 1974.

RECOMMENDED LISTENING

Marley's greatest hits album *Legend* (1984) is the most obvious starting block for an exploration of Reggae music. The songs are infectious with strong melodies and were recorded and mixed in the style of rock records of their day. Some may question this music's authenticity, so listen to artists like Toots And The Maytals (whose single 'Do The Reggay' is said to have given the genre its name) and Jimmy Cliff ('The Harder They Come') to gain a broader picture.

Rasta Monkey

Noam Lederman

SONG TITLE: MAIDEN VOYAGE

GENRE: INDIE ROCK

TEMPO: 130 BPM

KEY: E MAJOR

COMPOSER: JOE BENNETT

PERSONNEL: STUART RYAN (GTR)

HENRY THOMAS (BASS)

NOAM LEDERMAN (DRUMS)

JOE BENNETT (KEYS)

OVERVIEW

'Maiden Voyage' is an Indie Rock track influenced by bands like Coldplay, Arcarde Fire and The Killers.

THE BIGGER PICTURE

Bands such as Colplay and The Killers have led something of a resurgence in the use of keyboards, with the dominance of the guitar as the instrument providing the main harmonic and rhythmic interest giving way to an increased role for keyboards and synths. As with any music featuring both guitars and keyboards, the parts for each instrument have to make allowance for the presence of another instrument operating in the same range.

The idea of using synthesizers and guitars as equal partners in a rock track is not new. The Beatles did it in the late 1960s using early Moog synths. Prog rock bands of the 1970s such as Yes and Genesis used the synthesizer, electric piano or organ to share melodic duties with the guitar and vocal. These days, of course, many keyboard sounds are provided by computers, with bands such as Coldplay and The Killers frequently using a laptop on stage.

RECOMMENDED LISTENING

The Beatles' songs 'I Want You (She's So Heavy)' and 'Here Comes The Sun' include some great guitar/synth tradeoff lines. The Who's guitarist, Pete Townshend, plays some wonderful, sparse rhythm guitar between the synth lines on 'Who Are You', 'Love Reign O'er Me' and 'Won't Get Fooled Again'. For other examples of guitar/keyboard sparring, check out Van Halen's 'Jump', The Killers' 'Somebody Told Me' or Coldplay's 'Fix You'.

Maiden Voyage

Joe Bennett

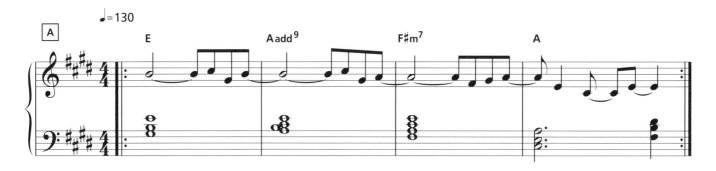

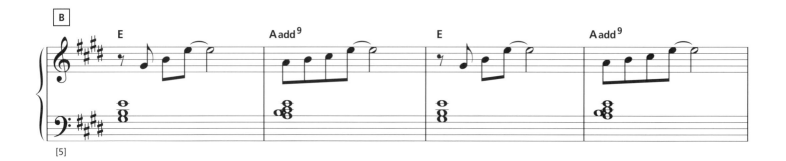

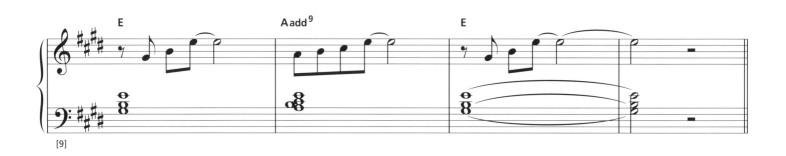

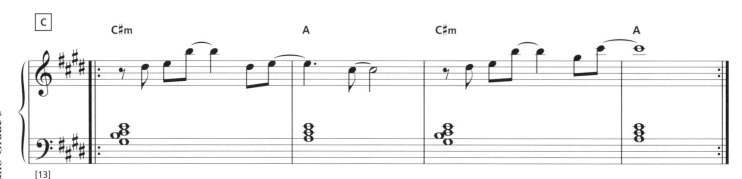

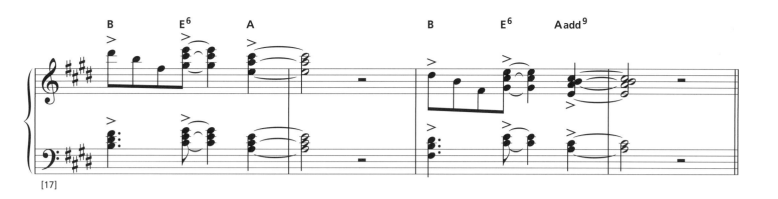

[17]

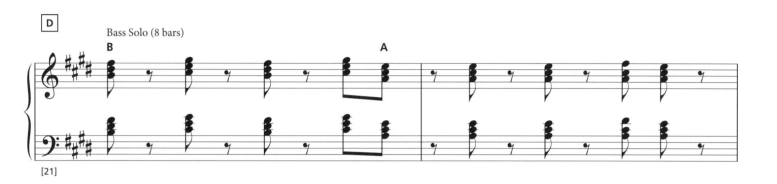

D   Bass Solo (8 bars)

[21]

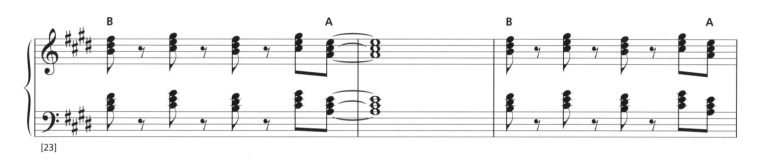

[23]

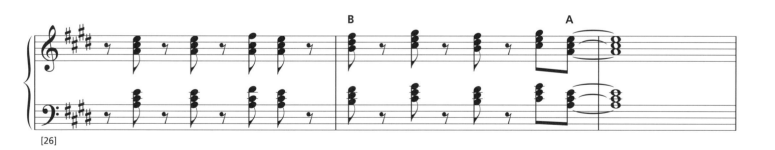

[26]

E

[29]

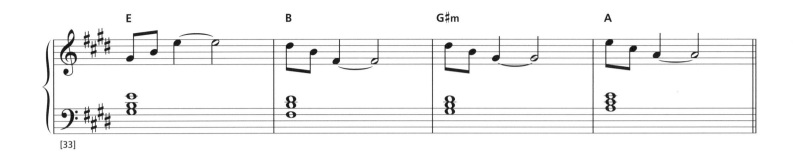

[33]

F

Piano Solo (8 bars)

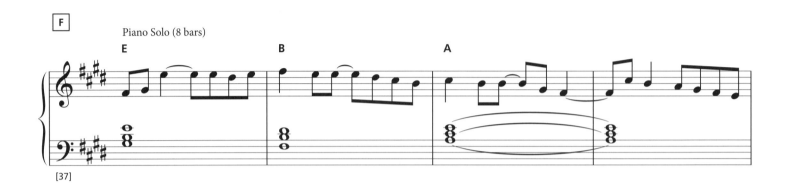

[37]

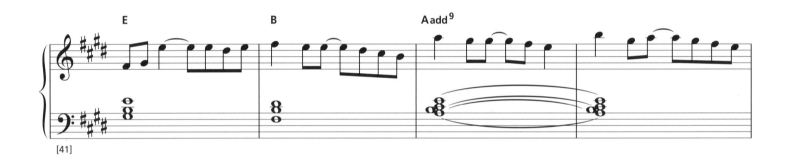

[41]

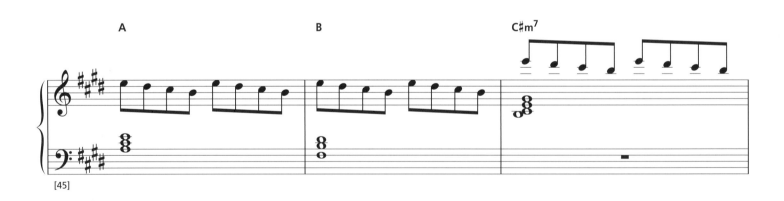

[45]

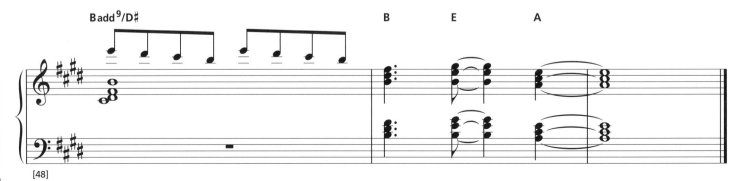

[48]

Technical Exercises

In this section, you will be asked to play a selection of exercises drawn from each of the groups below. The examiner will be looking for the speed of your response and will also give credit for the level of your musicality.

All exercises need to be played:
- Ascending and descending, in the keys, octaves and tempos shown.
- Hands together except for chromatic scales and the extended arpeggio which need to be played hands separately.
- In either swung or straight feel, as directed by the examiner.

You can use your book in the exam for Groups A and B. Group C must be performed from memory.

Note that Groups A and B need to be played to a click and any fingerings shown are suggestions only.

Group A: Scales
The tempo for this group is ♩ = 80 bpm.

1. A major scale

2. A major scale | contrary motion

3. E♭ major scale

4. E♭ major scale | contrary motion

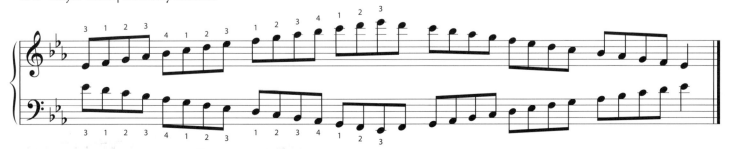

5. F♯ natural minor scale

6. C natural minor scale

7. F♯ harmonic minor scale

8. C harmonic minor scale

9. C lydian scale

10. Chromatic scale on A | right hand

11. Chromatic scale on A | left hand

12. Chromatic scale on E♭ | right hand

13. Chromatic scale on E♭ | left hand

Group B: Arpeggios
The tempo for this group is ♩ = 69 bpm.

1. A major arpeggio

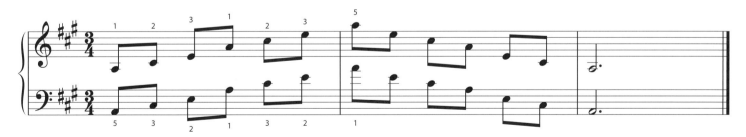

2. E♭ major arpeggio

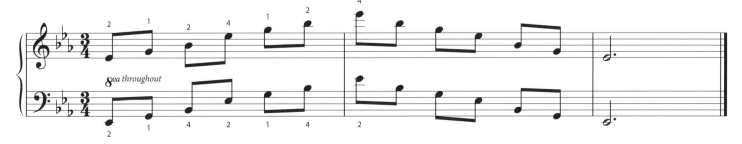

3. F♯ minor arpeggio

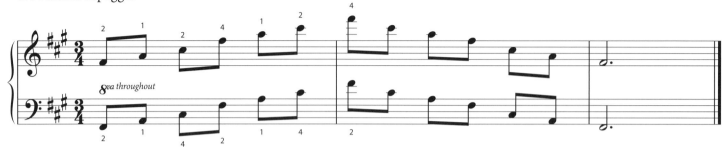

4. C minor arpeggio

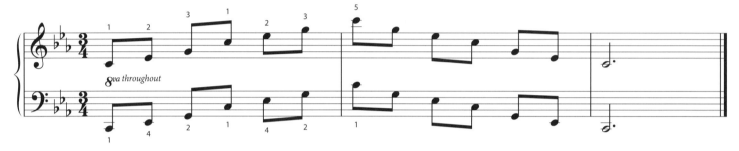

5. C major seventh (Cmaj^7) arpeggio

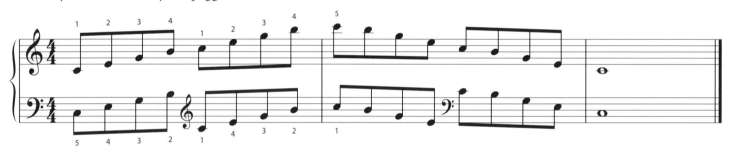

6. C major ninth sharp eleven (Cmaj$^{9\sharp11}$) arpeggio | right hand

7. C major ninth sharp eleven (Cmaj$^{9\sharp11}$) arpeggio | left hand

Group C: Chord Voicings

In the exam you will be asked to play, from memory, your choice of one chord voicing from each of the following exercises, without the aid of a backing track or metronome. However, for practice purposes a demonstration of the chords played to a metronome click is available in the downloadable audio.

1. C major 7

2. C dominant 9 sus 4

Sight Reading

In this section you have a choice between either a sight reading test or an improvisation and interpretation test (see facing page).

The examiner will ask you which one you wish to choose before commencing. Once you have decided you cannot change your mind.

In the sight reading test, the examiner will give you a 4–8 bar melody in the key of E♭ major or A major. You will first be given 90 seconds to practise, after which the examiner will play the backing track twice. The first time is for you to practise and the second time is for you to perform the final version for the exam. For each playthrough, the backing track will begin with a one bar count-in. The tempo is ♩=60–95.

During the practice time, you will be given the choice of a metronome click throughout or a one bar count-in at the beginning.

The backing track is continuous, so once the first playthrough has finished, the count-in of the second playing will start immediately.

Sight Reading | Example 1

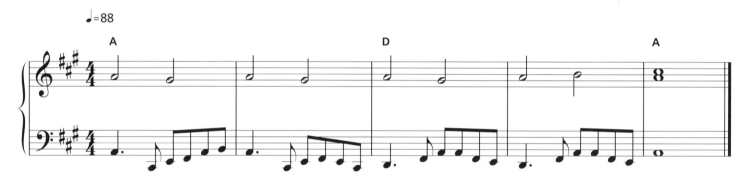

Please note: The test shown is an example. The examiner will give you a different version in the exam.

Sight Reading | Example 2

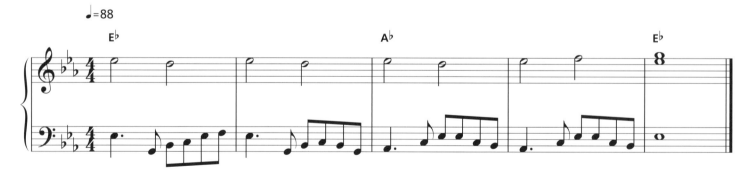

Please note: The test shown is an example. The examiner will give you a different version in the exam.

Improvisation & Interpretation

In the improvisation and interpretation test, the examiner will give you a 4–8 bar chord progression in the key of E♭ major or A major. You will first be given 90 seconds to practise, after which the examiner will play the backing track twice. The first time is for you to practise and the second time is for you to perform the final version for the exam. For each playthrough, the backing track will begin with a one bar count-in. The tempo is ♩=60–95.

During the practice time, you will be given the choice of a metronome click throughout or a one bar count-in at the beginning.

The backing track is continuous, so once the first playthrough has finished, the count-in of the second playing will start immediately.

You are only required to improvise single note melodies, with either right or left hand. It is permissible to play chord voicings, but please note you will only be marked on melodic content.

Improvisation & Interpretation | Example 1

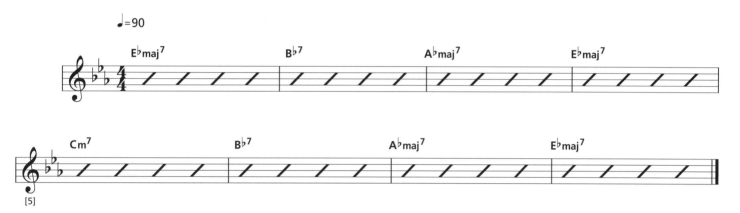

Please note: The test shown is an example. The examiner will give you a different version in the exam.

Improvisation & Interpretation | Example 2

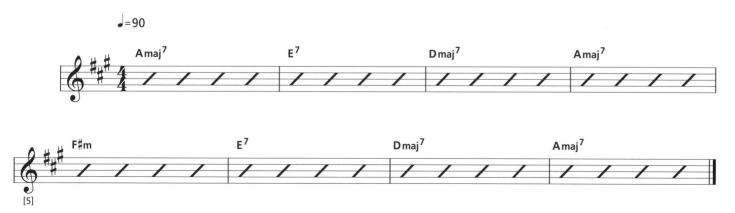

Please note: The test shown is an example. The examiner will give you a different version in the exam.

Ear Tests

In this section, there are two ear tests:
- Melodic Recall
- Chord Recognition

You will find one example of each type of test printed below and you will need perform both of them in the exam.

Test 1: Melodic Recall

The examiner will play you a 2 bar diatonic melody in the key of C major with a range up to a fifth. The first note will be the root note. You will hear the test twice, each time with a one bar count-in, then you will hear a further one bar count-in after which you will need to play the melody to the click. The tempo is ♩=95 bpm.

It is acceptable to play over the track as it is being played as well as practising after the second playthough. The length of time available after the second playthrough is pre-recorded on the audio track so the count-in may begin while you are still practising.

Please note: The test shown is an example. The examiner will give you a different version in the exam.

Test 2: Chord Recognition

The examiner will play you a sequence of chords, each with a C root note. You will hear the chord sequence twice, each time with a one bar count-in. You will then be asked to identify the chord quality of two of the chords, from a choice of major, minor, diminished, augmented, dominant 7th and major 7th. The tempo is ♩=95 bpm.

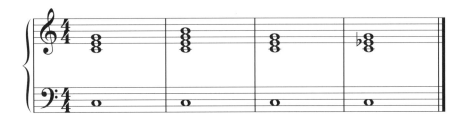

Please note: The test shown is an example. The examiner will give you a different version in the exam.

General Musicianship Questions

The final part of your exam is the General Musicianship Questions section, which features 5 questions relating to one of your choice of the performance pieces.

1. You will be asked a question relating to the harmony from a section of one of your pieces.

2. You will be asked a question relating to the melody in a section of one of your pieces.

3. You will be asked a question relating to the rhythms used in a section of one of your pieces.

4. You will be asked a question relating to the technical requirements of one of your pieces.

5. You will be asked a question relating to the genre of one of your pieces.

Entering Rockschool Exams

Entering a Rockschool exam is easy, just go online and follow our simple six step process. All details for entering online, dates, fees, regulations and Free Choice pieces can be found at *www.rslawards.com*

- All candidates should ensure they bring their own Grade syllabus book to the exam or have their KR app ready and the full book downloaded.

- All Grade 6–8 candidates must ensure that they bring valid photo ID to their exam.

- Candidates will receive their exam results (and certificates if applicable) a maximum of 3 weeks after their exam. If nothing has been received after this time then please call +44 (0)845 460 4747 or email to *info@rslawards.com*

Marking Schemes

Grade Exams | Debut to Grade 5 *

ELEMENT	PASS	MERIT	DISTINCTION
Performance Piece 1	12–14 out of 20	15–17 out of 20	18+ out of 20
Performance Piece 2	12–14 out of 20	15–17 out of 20	18+ out of 20
Performance Piece 3	12–14 out of 20	15–17 out of 20	18+ out of 20
Technical Exercises	9–10 out of 15	11–12 out of 15	13+ out of 15
Sight Reading *or* Improvisation & Interpretation	6 out of 10	7–8 out of 10	9+ out of 10
Ear Tests	6 out of 10	7–8 out of 10	9+ out of 10
General Musicianship Questions	3 out of 5	4 out of 5	5 out of 5
TOTAL MARKS	**60%+**	**74%+**	**90%+**

Grade Exams | Grades 6–8

ELEMENT	PASS	MERIT	DISTINCTION
Performance Piece 1	12–14 out of 20	15–17 out of 20	18+ out of 20
Performance Piece 2	12–14 out of 20	15–17 out of 20	18+ out of 20
Performance Piece 3	12–14 out of 20	15–17 out of 20	18+ out of 20
Technical Exercises	9–10 out of 15	11–12 out of 15	13+ out of 15
Quick Study Piece	6 out of 10	7–8 out of 10	9+ out of 10
Ear Tests	6 out of 10	7–8 out of 10	9+ out of 10
General Musicianship Questions	3 out of 5	4 out of 5	5 out of 5
TOTAL MARKS	**60%+**	**74%+**	**90%+**

Performance Certificates | Debut to Grade 8 *

ELEMENT	PASS	MERIT	DISTINCTION
Performance Piece 1	12–14 out of 20	15–17 out of 20	18+ out of 20
Performance Piece 2	12–14 out of 20	15–17 out of 20	18+ out of 20
Performance Piece 3	12–14 out of 20	15–17 out of 20	18+ out of 20
Performance Piece 4	12–14 out of 20	15–17 out of 20	18+ out of 20
Performance Piece 5	12–14 out of 20	15–17 out of 20	18+ out of 20
TOTAL MARKS	**60%+**	**75%+**	**90%+**

* Note that there are no Debut Vocal exams.

Copyright Information

Unfaithful
(Eriksen/Hermansen/Smith)
Sony/ATV Music Publishing (UK) Limited/EMI Music Publishing Limited/Imagem Music.

Skyfall (from the Motion Picture Skyfall)
(Epworth/Adkins)
Universal Music Publishing Limited/EMI Music Publishing Limited.

(Sittin' On) The Dock Of The Bay
(Redding/Cropper)
Warner/Chappell Music Limited/Rondor Music International.

mcps

INTRODUCING...

rockschool®

POPULAR MUSIC THEORY

The *essential* guide for rock & pop musicians

GRADES DEBUT–8

OUT NOW!

Discover more at
www.rslawards.com/theory

Enter online at
www.rslawards.com/enter-online